Beyoncé

Other books in the People in the News series:

Beyoncé

by Terri Dougherty

LUCENT BOOKS

An imprint of Thomson Gale, a part of The Thomson Corporation

Detroit • New York • San Francisco • New Haven, Conn. • Waterville, Maine • London

For more information, contact
Lucent Books
27500 Drake Rd.
Farmington Hills, MI 48331-3535
Or you can visit our Internet site at http://www.gale.com

LIBRARY OF CONGRESS CATALOGING-IN-PUBLICATION DATA

Dougherty, Terri.
Beyoncé / by Terri Dougherty.
    p. cm. — (People in the news)
Includes bibliographical references and index.
ISBN-13: 978-1-59018-929-0 (hardcover : alk. paper)
ISBN-10: 1-59018-929-9 (hardcover : alk. paper)
1. Knowles, Beyoncé—Juvenile literature. 2. Singers—United States—Biography—Juvenile literature. I. Title. II. Series: People in the news (San Diego, Calif.)
ML3930.K66D68 2007
782.42164'092—dc22
[B]
                                                          2006017088

Printed in the United States of America

Contents

F ame and celebrity are alluring. People are drawn to those who walk in fame's spotlight, whether they are known for great accomplishments or for notorious deeds. The lives of the famous pique public interest and attract attention, perhaps because their experiences seem in some ways so different from, yet in other ways so similar to, our own.

Newspapers, magazines, and television regularly capitalize on this fascination with celebrity by running profiles of famous people. For example, television programs such as *Entertainment Tonight* devote all of their programming to stories about entertainment and entertainers. Magazines such as *People* fill their pages with stories of the private lives of famous people. Even newspapers, newsmagazines, and television news frequently delve into the lives of well-known personalities. Despite the number of articles and programs, few provide more than a superficial glimpse at their subjects.

Lucent's People in the News series offers young readers a deeper look into the lives of today's newsmakers, the influences that have shaped them, and the impact they have had in their fields of endeavor and on other people's lives. The subjects of the series hail from many disciplines and walks of life. They include authors, musicians, athletes, political leaders, entertainers, entrepreneurs, and others who have made a mark on modern life and who, in many cases, will continue to do so for years to come.

These biographies are more than factual chronicles. Each book emphasizes the contributions, accomplishments, or deeds that have brought fame or notoriety to the individual and shows how that person has influenced modern life. Authors portray their subjects in a realistic, unsentimental light. For example, Bill Gates—the cofounder and chief executive officer of the software giant Microsoft—has been instrumental in making personal computers the most vital tool of the modern age. Few dispute his business savvy, his perseverance, or his technical expertise, yet critics say he is ruthless in his dealings with competitors and driven more by his desire to maintain Microsoft's dominance in the computer industry than by an interest in furthering technology.

In these books, young readers will encounter inspiring stories about real people who achieved success despite enormous obstacles. Oprah Winfrey—the most powerful, most watched, and wealthiest woman on television today—spent the first six years of her life in the care of her grandparents while her unwed mother sought work and a better life elsewhere. Her adolescence was colored by promiscuity, pregnancy at age fourteen, rape, and sexual abuse.

Each author documents and supports his or her work with an array of primary and secondary source quotations taken from diaries, letters, speeches, and interviews. All quotes are footnoted to show readers exactly how and where biographers derive their information and provide guidance for further research. The quotations enliven the text by giving readers eyewitness views of the life and accomplishments of each person covered in the People in the News series.

In addition, each book in the series includes photographs, annotated bibliographies, timelines, and comprehensive indexes. For both the casual reader and the student researcher, the People in the News series offers insight into the lives of today's newsmakers—people who shape the way we live, work, and play in the modern age.

Focused on Stardom

Beyoncé Knowles has known since she was a child that she wanted to be a performer and has devoted her life to becoming a superstar. Her Grammy Award–winning songs, glamorous looks, and hip-shaking dance moves have made her so well-known that her first name alone brings recognition. She has sold more than 40 million albums and is famous around the world as a singer, dancer, and, more recently, actress. While beauty and talent have played a role in bringing Beyoncé to this level of fame, her success is due to more than looks and singing ability. Dedication to improving herself and a drive to succeed have helped her become a star.

Beyoncé has not become an accomplished performer on her own. Her parents have been devoted to her dream as well and refocused their own careers to help their daughter with hers. When Beyoncé showed a talent for performing at a young age, it was her father who set up a practice and performance schedule for her. He coached his daughter in interviewing techniques and groomed her to handle the public demands of being a celebrity. He left his job to manage Beyoncé's career while she was still a young teen. This move resulted in financial difficulties for the family, who all made sacrifices as Beyoncé pursued her dreams of stardom.

While Beyoncé has achieved success as a performer, fame has not made her life easier. Frequent practices and performances meant that her childhood was far from traditional. Since she was a young teen, she has had to worry constantly about her diet and watch her weight. Sleep is often a luxury, as she moves from

Beyoncé performs at President George W. Bush's inauguration in 2001.

rehearsals to performances, interviews, and other public appearances. While her dedication to her career has brought her financial success, luxurious surroundings, and recognition for her talent, it has also forced her to give up some of her free time and privacy.

As a longtime participant in a highly competitive field, Beyoncé has been through her share of personality conflicts as well. She first gained recognition as the lead singer of the group Destiny's Child. The group began as a close-knit quartet of girls focused on recording songs and performing, but gradually Beyoncé moved to the forefront. Jealousy and competition began to divide the group, and the fact that Beyoncé's father was the group's manager led to suspicions that he was favoring his daughter. Although Beyoncé continually denied that she was trying to become famous at the others' expense, the more success the group achieved, the more divided the members became. Two of them left, and after a tumultuous time, the group reorganized as a trio, but not before Beyoncé became depressed over the media attention that resulted from the group's differences.

In spite of Beyoncé's worries, however, her reputation and the group's popularity were only improved by the publicity surrounding the group's changes. Beyoncé became the undisputed leader of the highly successful trio of female singers and made the transition to solo star and fledgling actress. Her reputation has been enhanced by her ability to avoid tabloid scandals and cultivate a wholesome image. She has turned this image into a business, with product promotions and her own perfume and clothing line. As she remains committed to her career, she is focusing on achieving the same level of accomplishment as an actress that she has found as a singer. She has been striving for success since she was seven years old and has no intention of stopping now, as every new song and acting role presents a new challenge.

Chapter 1

Groomed for Success

At an early age, Beyoncé Knowles showed a talent for singing and an interest in performing. While she was a shy girl at school, a different side of her personality emerged onstage. Her talent was first noticed in an after-school dance class and burst forth in public at a talent show. When her parents realized the extent of their daughter's gift, they encouraged her to continue performing.

Beyoncé's parents nurtured their daughter's love for singing and dancing by entering her in local talent shows. This led to membership in an all-girls singing group, a loss on a nationally televised talent competition, and the formation of the group that would later become Destiny's Child. Her father became the group's manager and encouraged Beyoncé to practice as he groomed his daughter for stardom. Even as a child, Beyoncé had a goal of becoming a singer and was willing to put in time and effort to hone her skills. With her father at the helm of her career, she was on her way to achieving her dream.

Successful Family

Beyoncé Giselle Knowles was born in Houston, Texas, on September 4, 1981. Her unconventional name was the result of an agreement between her parents, who each chose one of their daughter's names. Her father, Mathew Knowles, selected the middle name, and her mother, Tina Knowles, chose the first name.

Glistening highrise buildings shape the skyline of Houston, Texas, birthplace of Beyoncé.

Tina Knowles named her daughter Beyoncé because that had been her maiden name.

In 1986, Beyoncé's younger sister, Solange, was born. The Knowles family lived a comfortable life in Houston. Mathew Knowles sold medical equipment such as MRI and CT scanning machines, while Tina Knowles owned and operated a successful hair salon. The family could afford a nice home and had a housekeeper to help keep it looking its best. When it was time for Beyoncé to enter kindergarten, she went to a private school. She spent most of her elementary years at Saint James and Saint Mary's schools.

Beyoncé was a quiet student, rarely speaking up in class. Her unusual name made for some uncomfortable moments for the introverted girl. It was often mispronounced, and when that happened too often she would become upset. "As a kid, I hated my name," Beyoncé says. "I ran around screaming, 'Fools, it rhymes with fiancee.'"[1]

Usually, however, Beyoncé avoided drawing attention to herself. She even tried to dress plainly so she would not stand out. "No one would have believed that my mom owned her own beauty salon," she says, "because I went out of my way not to look too pretty."[2]

Blossoming Onstage

Because Beyoncé was so shy, her parents enrolled her in dance class to help her learn to be more comfortable around other children. The class was held every day after school, and it was there

Beyoncé's parents, Mathew and Tina Knowles (pictured), enrolled their daughter in a dance class at age six to help her overcome her shyness.

that Beyoncé's talent as a performer emerged. The shyness that Beyoncé felt in class evaporated when she was dancing.

Beyoncé's dance teacher was the first to notice her talent. She told Tina and Mathew Knowles that there was something special about their daughter, but initially Beyoncé's parents did not realize how significant their daughter's talent was. "You know, everyone thinks their child is special, so I just said O.K.,'"[3] Tina Knowles recalls.

Her opinion changed when she saw Beyoncé sing John Lennon's song "Imagine" in a school talent show when Beyoncé was about seven years old. A few days before the show, Beyoncé's father had explained the meaning of the song, which asks listeners to imagine a peaceful world. When she was onstage, Beyoncé was able to convey that meaning to the crowd. When Tina and Mathew Knowles saw the emotion their daughter was able to pour into the song, they realized what Beyoncé's dance teacher had been talking about. "When she got onstage she was just a different kid; she was so confident and she looked so happy and we were like,

Last Name, First Name

When Beyoncé's mother decided to give her daughter her maiden name, one of the people who was skeptical about the choice was Beyoncé's grandfather. Tina Knowles decided to name her daughter Beyoncé because only one of her brothers had a son, and she wanted the family name to be carried on. Her father, however, was not sure this was a good idea. "My family was not happy," Tina Knowles said. "My Dad said she's gonna be really mad at you because that's a last name. And I'm like it's not a last name to anybody but you guys."

Quoted in Toure, "A Woman Possessed," *Rolling Stone*, March 4, 2004, p. 38.

'Who is that?' After that, there was no stopping her—she was obsessed,"[4] Tina Knowles admits.

Immediately after her performance, Beyoncé knew she had done well. In her mind, she was already the winner. She did not even want to wait and see how the rest of the performers did. She told her mom she was ready to get her trophy and go home.

Talent Show Champ

Beyoncé did indeed win the contest, and afterward she was eager to perform again. She sang and danced at home, using chairs and tables as stages. She loved the energy that arose inside her when she was performing. She did not feel bashful when she was expressing herself on a stage.

Because Beyoncé loved performing so much, her parents entered her in a number of children's talent contests. The contests included both beauty and talent portions, and for the beauty part of the contests Beyoncé dressed in frilly gowns and had her long hair styled. She hated dressing up but endured the walk down the runway in front of the judges for the opportunity to sing.

Beyoncé was very successful in the contests. After a year of competition, her room was filled with the trophies and crowns she had won. Her parents began to realize the depth of her talent and continued to look for ways for her to display it.

Girl's Tyme

In 1990, Beyoncé's parents took her to an event in Houston called the People's Workshop. There, singers and dancers had the opportunity to perform in front of talent scouts. Beyoncé's talent stood out to a pair of women in the audience, who asked her to try out for a group called Girl's Tyme. The all-girl group would perform at banquets and other events in the Houston area.

More than fifty girls auditioned, and nine-year-old Beyoncé was one of those accepted into the group. She had been performing alone until then, but she did not mind sharing the spotlight with the other group members. She said singing with others took some of the pressure off her.

The group's lineup was constantly changing; a new member was added when a girl left. As many as one hundred girls performed with the group at one time or another. One of the members of the group was LaTavia Roberson, a dancer who became friends with Beyoncé, and in 1991, Kelly Rowland joined Girl's Tyme.

New Sister

Kelly and Beyoncé saw each other at the group's frequent practices, and Kelly began spending more and more time at Beyoncé's house. Kelly had moved to Houston from Atlanta the previous year with her mother, Doris Lovett, who worked as a nanny. Lovett was a single parent who was struggling financially, and she and her daughter moved often.

Lovett wanted her daughter to have a more stable home, and she asked Tina and Mathew Knowles if they could care for Kelly. The Knowleses agreed, and Kelly and Beyoncé became roommates at the Knowles home. Beyoncé and Kelly got along well, but it took Beyoncé some time to get used to sharing her room, closet, and parents with Kelly. After a few months, however, the situation felt natural, and Kelly became like a sister to her. "I'm happy she moved in when we were both young—we weren't old enough to be that set in our ways," Beyoncé says. "In the beginning there may have been some awkwardness, and that's very normal, but it was nothing but good times once we got past that."[5]

Star Search

Beyoncé and Kelly shared a love for singing. Along with the other Girl's Tyme members, they performed at local events and submitted an audition tape to a television show called *Star Search*. The show, emceed by Ed McMahon, was a national talent competition that gave amateur performers a chance to be discovered. The show ran from 1983 to 1995 and was similar to the more recent television show *American Idol*.

The Right Look

As a young teen, Beyoncé struggled with how she looked. She had been chubby until about age ten, and she had to watch carefully what she ate so she would stay slim. Although she was tempted by pizza, soda, and junk food, she tried to eat healthier foods instead.

Beyoncé realized that those sacrifices were necessary if she wanted to achieve her dream of being a professional singer. "At school, all the other kids in the cafeteria would be eating Ho Hos, and I'd have to sit there and sip soup," she says. "It's a shame that a kid would have to worry about her weight, but I was trying to get a record deal and that was a reality."

Beyoncé Knowles, Kelly Rowland, Michelle Williams, and James Patrick Herman, *Soul Survivors: The Official Autobiography of Destiny's Child*. New York: HarperCollins, 2002, p. 77.

Six members of Girl's Tyme, three singers and three dancers, all of whom were ten or eleven years old, practiced for months for their appearance on the show in 1992. The girls were confident they would win. Wearing jean shorts and satin jackets, they performed a rap song for their big number. The girls gave it their all; however, they did not impress the judges. Looking back on the experience years later, Beyoncé said the song did not allow the group to show the full extent of their talent. They lost to a rock band and were devastated. They managed to keep their composure on camera but could not hide their grief for long. "We went backstage and bawled,"[6] Beyoncé recalls.

Regrouping

Despite the loss, Beyoncé's father still saw promise for the girls. He tried to boost their spirits by taking them to Disneyland the next day. However, after all their hard work, the letdown of the loss on *Star Search* had hit the girls hard. They were ready to leave show business behind.

Mathew Knowles encouraged the girls not to give up on their dreams. He proposed that he manage a new group that included several members of Girl's Tyme, including Beyoncé. Even though he had never worked in the music industry before, Knowles had drive, dedication, and a vision for what the group could become. He persuaded Beyoncé, Kelly, and LaTavia not to quit, and the three formed the core of the new group.

The group changed several times, with additional members and different names. At various times the girls called themselves Somethin' Fresh, Borderline, Cliché, the Dolls, and Destiny. The girls tried out a variety of musical styles, singing rhythm and blues, gospel, and hip-hop songs. A friend of Kelly's, LaToya Luckett, joined the group while it was calling itself Somethin' Fresh and stayed as its members pursued stardom.

Practice, Practice

The girls devoted themselves to perfecting their performance. They watched a tape of the *Star Search* program over and over again and identified the mistakes they had made. They drew up a list of improvements they needed to make, including learning new songs and routines. To make these improvements, they agreed to practice every day. They jogged to improve their endurance so they would not get tired while singing and dancing. They also vowed to learn to sing a cappella and worked with voice and dance coaches. Kelly later recalled that the girls were very critical of themselves at a young age. "Nothing ever seemed perfect to us. We were so strict, always critiquing ourselves, which is a good thing, but at the same time we missed out on a lot of our childhood."[7]

Even though rehearsing took up almost all of the girls' free time, Beyoncé made it clear that this was what she wanted to do. She says she did not have a harsh childhood, but rather was following her dream. "I didn't grow up poor," she says. "I went to private school; we had a very nice house, cars, a housekeeper. I wasn't doing this because I didn't have a choice, or to support the

In 1992, Girl's Tyme performed on the television talent show **Star Search,** *hosted by Ed McMahon (pictured).*

family, or because I had to get out of a bad situation. I was just determined; this is what I wanted to do so bad."[8]

Music was not a chore for Beyoncé; it was something she loved. In addition to singing, she enjoyed listening to the music her parents had around the house. Anita Baker and Donny Hathaway were some of her mother's favorites, so Beyoncé became familiar with their songs. When her father bought a collection of classic songs on the Motown label, Beyoncé was fascinated by them.

Beyoncé performs in Las Vegas in 1999. As a child, she practiced singing and dancing for hours every day.

Sacrifices

Beyoncé and the other girls attended their own version of summer camp for three years as they polished their musical talents. As the group's manager, Knowles set the girls' schedule. The girls began their days with a 3-mile run (4.83km) and then practiced their singing and dancing for hours. To get a taste for choreography, they watched videos of Motown groups such as the Supremes and the Jackson Five. Beyoncé especially liked watching the Supremes and admired their glamour and poise.

Knowles respected the way Berry Gordy, the founder of the Motown record label, had groomed stars such as the Supremes. Gordy had made sure his singers had a look and demeanor that were polished and professional. Knowles wanted his daughter and

The glamour and style of the Supremes, shown here in a 1967 performance, inspired Beyoncé.

the other members of the group to have a similar image, so their practice schedule included instruction in poise as well as singing and dancing. He also felt they should learn to act properly during interviews, so they practiced being interviewed by the press.

The girls also needed to be comfortable performing in front of people, so Knowles looked for places for them to present their act. His goal was to have them perform each week during the school year and twice a week in the summer. Although her father's training schedule meant she spent a great deal of time practicing and performing, Beyoncé did not complain. She was dedicated to improving, as she knew it could all pay off with a recording contract.

The original members of Beyoncé's singing group included (left to right) Beyoncé, Kelly Rowland, LaTavia Roberson, and LaToya Luckett.

The entire Knowles family made sacrifices to give Beyoncé the chance to reach her potential as a performer. Mathew Knowles left his job as a successful medical equipment salesman to manage his daughter's career, and Tina Knowles cut back on her hair salon business to become the group's stylist and clothing designer. Beyoncé's father booked appearances for the girls, and her mother designed and made their costumes.

Balancing Act

Tina Knowles was supportive of her daughter's career, but she also realized that singing and dancing were not all a child should be doing. While Mathew Knowles prepared his daughter to perform professionally, her mother made sure that she enjoyed some of the fun of childhood. "My mother is the balance," Beyoncé says. "She's very strong and will say whatever she feels and protects me always, but she always kept me a normal kid."[9] Beyoncé recognized that her father meant well with his intensive practice schedule, but she also realized that he thought of doing little else. Beyoncé's mother knew the importance of allowing time for other activities and had Beyoncé make time for fun activities such as slumber parties with her friends. "My father was more focused," Beyoncé said. "He wanted it for me and did everything because he's my father and wanted me to be happy, but he's a workaholic."[10]

Keeping Quiet

Although singing, dancing, and performing were what Beyoncé loved to do, she kept her dreams hidden from her classmates. She felt some of the other children already thought she was snobbish because she was shy, and she did not want them to think she was an egotistical performer. She also did not want to have to prove to people that she was a good singer. "That's part of the reason why I was so quiet, because I felt like I would have to prove myself and I didn't know what to say, so I would rather not say anything," she says. "I would just smile and be quiet."[11]

Biblical Inspiration

The "Destiny" half of the name Destiny's Child came from the Bible, from a verse in the Book of Isaiah. "Whenever I'm confused about something I ask God to reveal the answers to my questions, and he does," Beyoncé says. "That's how we found our name—we opened up the Bible, and the word 'destiny' was right there."

About six months after the group changed its name to Destiny, it was asked to contribute a song to the *Men in Black* soundtrack. There were too many other groups called Destiny, so "Child" was added to the group's name to set it apart.

Quoted in Lorraine Bracco, "Destiny's Child," *Interview*, August 2001, p. 84.

Beyoncé transferred to her first public school, Welch Middle School, when she was in eighth grade. While she felt excited and mature to be going to a new school, she was also worried about how she would be treated by her classmates. A cousin who went to another public school warned her that other girls might cut her long hair off if they became jealous of her. Beyoncé's solution was to keep quiet. "The first day I walked into class, I was trying to be invisible, because I didn't want anybody to beat me up or talk bad about me,"[12] she says.

Family Difficulties

Around this time, Beyoncé encountered some personal troubles at home as well. After her father quit his job to manage the group, the family ran into financial difficulties. When Beyoncé was fourteen, the stress of managing the group and taking care of his family became especially difficult for Mathew, and he and Tina separated for a time.

Beyoncé, Solange, and Kelly moved to a small apartment with Tina. Although she was worried, Beyoncé did not know exactly what was going on. All she knew for sure was that she had moved into a smaller home and the family had sold one of its cars.

Beyoncé did not know where her father was for a time. Her mother was depressed, and the family had little money. The situation was grim, but the bad times did not last long. After about six months, Beyoncé's parents reunited, and Mathew Knowles again became a driving force in his daughter's life and career.

Beyoncé's entire family continued to support and encourage her as she pursued her goal of becoming a performer. The shy girl who was still hesitant to speak up in class found freedom from her bashful nature when she was singing and dancing. She thrived onstage and was willing to sacrifice her free time for the opportunity to perform. Even as a preteen, Beyoncé already showed the drive and dedication she would need to become a star.

Chapter 2

Child's Play

Under her father's guidance, Beyoncé was polishing her talent. She and the other girls in the group had the goal of signing a recording contract with a record producer, and they practiced relentlessly to make it happen. Success would come, but not without both hard work and disappointment.

Beyoncé's father learned some lessons as he navigated the group's career. Persuading a record company to sign the group to a contract would be one thing, and getting the company to back the group with time in the recording studio would be another. It took more than one try before Beyoncé and the group had a record company willing to support them, but once they did, Beyoncé was on her way to stardom.

Private Audition

Beyoncé, Kelly Rowland, LaTavia Roberson, and LaToya Luckett practiced in the living room of the Knowles home to polish their act and did some traveling to try to attract the notice of music industry executives. They went to talent shows and competitions in San Francisco and Oakland and also spent several months in San Francisco making a demo tape to send to record industry executives. The young girls were determined to succeed and were

Beyoncé and her group worked hard to get a record contract.

so focused on landing a record deal that they did not take time to enjoy their travels. They saw California only as a place where they could possibly sign a record deal, and they did not take time to see the sights or enjoy the scenery.

It was at home in Houston rather than in California, however, that the girls had their first chance at signing a recording contract. Knowles eventually succeeded in persuading a representative from Columbia Records, Teresa LaBarbera Whites, to listen to the group in a private audition. A good performance could result in a record deal for the girls, and he wanted them to take it seriously. He warned them not to go swimming the day before the audition, as he feared it would affect their voices. The young girls could not resist an offer to swim, however, and the day before the audition, they played in the pool at a friend's home.

Sure enough, on the day of the audition, Beyoncé's nose was clogged. That was not the group's only problem, however. Beyoncé was nervous, and her jitters rubbed off on the other girls, lessening the entire group's performance. Knowles knew the girls could

Style Problems

Destiny's Child became known for the stylish outfits Tina Knowles designed, but Beyoncé admitted that when she was fourteen, her taste in fashion left something to be desired. She was a tomboy who preferred platform sneakers to high heels. "My style back then could best be described as bad," she says. "I wore a lot of platform tennis shoes, little baby tees, jeans, gold chains and big hoop earrings."

Beyoncé Knowles, Kelly Rowland, Michelle Williams, and James Patrick Herman, *Soul Survivors: The Official Autobiography of Destiny's Child*. New York: HarperCollins, 2002, p. 80.

do better, and he even stopped them in the middle of a song and had them start over. Although the group did not sound its best, Knowles's efforts showed Whites that the girls had discipline and guidance. Despite the less-than-stellar performance, Whites and Columbia showed some interest in the group. Before things reached the contract signing stage, however, the girls had another chance to demonstrate their talent.

Recording Contract

Not long after performing for Whites at the private audition, the girls performed in a public event called Black Expo. The event gave people from the recording industry an opportunity to hear new talent. In the audience was songwriter and producer Daryl Simmons of Silent Partner Productions, who was impressed by the group. His company was connected with Elektra Records, and he was in a position to offer Knowles and the group the contract they had been hoping for.

Suddenly, the group had interest from two music companies at once, as Knowles was also discussing a contract with Whites and Columbia. After weighing the two offers, he decided to work with Simmons's Silent Partner Productions, which had studios in Atlanta. Using the name the Dolls, the quartet prepared to make its first album.

Disappointment

Several months after signing the contract, the girls moved to Atlanta to begin recording. LaTavia Roberson's mother was the chaperone for the group, and at age fourteen Beyoncé was away from her parents for the first time. The girls lived in the basement of a home owned by Simmons's assistant, and they slept on a couch and cots. In the mornings they were tutored, and in the afternoons they spent time in the recording studio.

Beyoncé initially missed her parents, but she soon began to enjoy the freedom being in Atlanta offered. The girls received $150 per week and spent much of it on clothes. When they were

Beyoncé and her group moved to Atlanta, Georgia (pictured), to record an album but were dropped by their label shortly after recording started.

not recording or studying, Beyoncé and her friends were usually at the city's malls.

The freedom did not last long, however. Shortly after the group began recording, and eight months after signing their first record contract, they were dropped by the label. The girls were shocked and let down. Simmons, who also worked with Babyface and Dru Hill, admitted he had taken on too many projects and did not have enough time to devote to the girls' effort. "Honestly, I wasn't prepared," he said. "I didn't come through. We may have recorded one or two things, but I couldn't tell you what they sounded like."[13]

Beyoncé had received a small taste of what a musical career would be like, but nothing more. She and the other girls had moved to Atlanta full of hope but left disappointed. Again, it seemed, their hard work had been for nothing. "We felt like our life was over," Beyoncé says. "We thought we would never get signed again."[14]

All in the Family

With her mother and father both intensely involved in her career, fourteen-year-old Beyoncé had a great deal riding on her shoulders. If she succeeded as a performer, the family did well. If she failed, the entire family suffered.

Beyoncé learned to cope with the pressure by realizing that if her musical aspirations did not pan out, her parents could go back to other careers. Her mother ran a successful hair salon, and her father had college degrees and business experience. "They didn't give up everything because that was our only hope to get us out of the ghetto," she says. "So I realized I didn't have to have that pressure because they're going to be successful regardless of what they do."

Tina and Mathew Knowles had their own careers before Beyoncé began singing professionally.

Quoted in Toure, "A Woman Possessed," *Rolling Stone*, March 4, 2004, p. 38.

Another Chance

Despite the discouraging experience, Mathew Knowles again rallied Beyoncé and the others, reminding them that another record contract was a possibility. Rather than letting the group disband, Knowles redoubled his efforts to get it signed to a record deal. "My parents let us mope around the house for a couple of weeks, and that's when my dad switched into high gear,"[15] Beyoncé says.

Knowles convinced the girls that the setback would only make the group stronger. He told them not to worry, and he got back in touch with the representative from Columbia Records, Teresa LaBarbera Whites. She was still interested in the group and asked them to come to New York City to meet with her. There they had another audition, this time in front of Whites and other industry executives. Singing without backup instruments, they performed "Are You Ready?" and "Ain't No Sunshine."

Singing in front of an audience that could hand them a music career or send them back into anonymity was an intimidating experience for the young girls. "It felt too intimate—being that close and having to make eye contact was very scary," Beyoncé recalls. "We knew that it might be our last chance, so we couldn't mess it up."[16]

After the performance the executives' blank expressions gave no indication whether the girls would be signed or not. The group returned to Houston uncertain if they had made a good impression, and they had to spend a few nerve-racking weeks waiting. The good news came while they were all at Tina Knowles's hair salon. They were handed an envelope, and inside was the contract. "We started screaming and crying right in the middle of the salon," Beyoncé recalls. "The ladies with their heads under the dryers looked at us like we were crazy."[17]

Destiny's Child

The girls signed their contract with Columbia Records in 1996 and called their group Destiny. They soon set to work on their first recording and were asked to contribute a song to the soundtrack for the movie *Men in Black*. Now that the group was going to be establishing itself on an album for the first time, Knowles wanted to make sure its name would stand out. He did not want it to be something that was too ordinary, so he added "Child" to the group's name after he found that many other groups were also called Destiny.

The group released "Killing Time" for the *Men in Black* soundtrack in 1997, and the next year released the single "No, No, No." The song was recorded in two versions, a slow version and a fast remix. The group credited producer Wyclef Jean with realizing that the song sounded good with a faster beat. Because time in the studio was expensive and limited, Jean wanted Beyoncé to

*Destiny's Child recorded a song for the **Men in Black** soundtrack in 1996.*

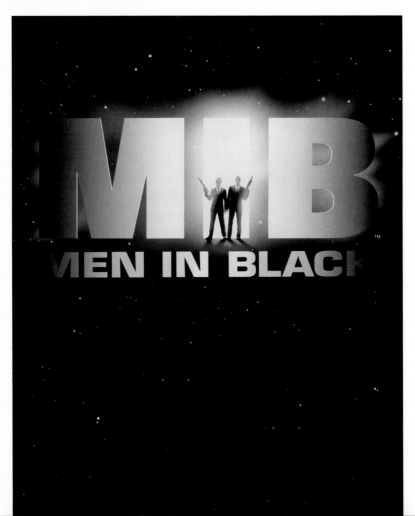

hurry and do the vocal track. As a joke, Beyoncé started singing the lyrics quickly, and the producer heard something he liked. "That was the first song we sang really fast, and it started as a joke," Beyoncé remembers. "I was playing around, and Wyclef was like, 'That's hot! You need to do it like that!'"[18]

The producer was right. Released in 1997 when Beyoncé was sixteen, "No, No, No" became the group's first big hit. It topped *Billboard*'s R&B singles chart in 1998 and made it to number three on the Hot 100 chart. It also helped the group garner its first music industry award. At the Lady of Soul Awards in 1998, the group won the Best R&B/Soul or Rap New Artist award for "No, No, No."

Back in the Studio

The song "No, No, No" was part of the group's first album, *Destiny's Child*, which was released in 1998. The album was not an immediate hit, but after the group continued to have success, its sales topped 1 million copies. After its release, the group did not wait long to return to the recording studio. The teens were asked to contribute a song to the soundtrack for the movie *Why Do Fools Fall in Love?* so they recorded "Get the Bus."

The group soon began recording its second album, called *The Writing's on the Wall*, and this time they were ready to take control. A number of producers had helped the group make its first album, and as a result, the group felt it lacked a signature sound. That problem was remedied with the second album, as Beyoncé and the other members, now more experienced, knew what they wanted to accomplish in the studio. "We weren't really nervous doing the second album," Beyoncé recalls. "We were just ready to do it because we weren't entirely satisfied with the first album. We had a lot of ideas for the second album. We grew up and had a lot to sing about."[19]

The long hours of practice and rehearsals had made Beyoncé a perfectionist who knew what she expected from Destiny's Child. She had firm opinions about how the group's songs should sound, and she wrote and produced some of the material for the group's

Yes, Yes, Yes

When "No, No, No" began getting radio airplay, Beyoncé was ecstatic. The first time she heard the song on the air, she and Rowland were in her Ford Explorer at Solange's school, where they had come to pick her up. The girls were excited to hear themselves on the radio at last. They were so thrilled that that they jumped out of the vehicle and began running around it, singing the song.

Solange was not sure what to make of her sister's actions until she got close enough to hear the music. Then she joined in. "She dropped her bag and books and started running around the car, too," Beyoncé remembered. "It was a really cool experience."

Beyoncé Knowles, Kelly Rowland, Michelle Williams, and James Patrick Herman, *Soul Survivors: The Official Autobiography of Destiny's Child*. New York: HarperCollins, 2002, p. 89.

second album. She did not let her youth or the fact that most of the other producers were male hold her back. "I was young, but it was a double struggle because I was also female," she said. "So when I earned respect, I felt extra good about it."[20]

Her efforts paid off; when the album was released in 1999, it debuted at number seven on the *Billboard* 200 album chart. The single "Bills, Bills, Bills" quickly went to the top ten and spent nine weeks as the number one single on the *Billboard* singles chart. The single "Say My Name" also became a hit, making it to the top of the Hot 100 and R&B singles charts.

The album featured a more cohesive sound than their first album had, showing the girls' growing confidence in their abilities. Reviewer Jeff Salamon noted that producer Kevin "She'kspere" Briggs used a number of rhythms to surround Beyoncé's voice and that she handled the changes adeptly. "That sort of trickery might undo a lesser talent, but Knowles maintains her composure—

Destiny's Child toured with the successful girl group, TLC, pictured here at the MTV Video Music Awards.

the distinctive cry in her voice. If she's not quite singing the blues, she's sure earned the right to."[21]

Success and Discord

The girls did not slow down after their second album was released. They became as dedicated to getting their name in front of audiences as they had been in securing a record contract. They made a number of appearances on radio stations to gain support and airplay for their songs. The group went on tour in the fall of 1999 with TLC, and their promotional efforts and catchy singles were rewarded with album sales. *The Writing's on the Wall* eventually sold more than 10 million copies.

Beyoncé and the group finally had the fame they had worked so hard for, but cracks were beginning to appear in the quartet's cohesiveness. The group's members had been united in pursuing success, but now that they were chart-topping artists, that goal no longer held them together. Moreover, although the group was becoming well-known, it was Beyoncé who was attracting the most attention. She was expanding her skills, becoming a producer and songwriter by age seventeen. As the group's lead singer, she was the one most frequently mentioned in reviews of their albums. Not all of the group members were happy with this turn of events.

The girls had worked diligently for years toward their dream of having a record contract. They had persevered when their first contract was canceled and were rewarded with another contract, a successful debut single, and an even more successful follow-up album. However, attention for the group and its lead singer was not enough for everyone. Although the group members had long sought fame, their success began to drive them apart.

Chapter 3

A New Destiny's Child

Two years after releasing its first single, Destiny's Child was selling millions of CDs; however, its increasing popularity was putting a strain on the quartet. The fact that Beyoncé was attracting more attention from the media than the others led to divisiveness. Kelly Rowland remained loyal to her friend, but LaTavia Roberson and LaToya Luckett began to feel as if they were being unfairly overshadowed.

The discord had unexpected positive consequences, however. While it made day-to-day life more difficult for the girls, it also brought the group new publicity. Their disharmony made the group newsworthy, and as the dissension grew, the group was increasingly covered by the media.

The fact that the group's problems were adding to its popularity was of little consolation to Beyoncé. She found it difficult to deal with criticism from her friends and the public. The public nature of the group's split was not easy for the singer, who did not want to be seen as a diva who stepped on the careers of her fellow singers. She had no desire to see the group break apart, but despite her feelings, the dissension with the group would eventually lead to changes in its membership. The experience would test Beyoncé's resolve and ability to carry on as a performer.

Minus Two

Luckett and Roberson's friendship with Beyoncé and Rowland began to crumble as egos, competition, and money began to get in the way of unity. Roberson and Luckett disliked the control Mathew Knowles had over the group, wanted more time in the spotlight, and felt Beyoncé was getting too much credit for the group's success. Beyoncé countered that she tried to give everyone in the group

Becoming Stronger

Beyoncé was still sensitive to what was said about her, even after Destiny's Child regained its stability and became more popular than ever. The painful accusations made by former group members continued to sting, and Beyoncé sometimes became angry over them, but she did not let them distract her from singing, acting, and performing. Beyoncé did not want to make enemies. Her focus instead was on her career.

The personnel changes Destiny's Child went through were difficult for Beyoncé, but they also taught her some lessons. "I've learned a lot about friendship and loyalty and life," she says. "All of us are so much stronger. Also, our lives have changed tremendously because we're now becoming these celebrities that we've always wanted to become."

Being a celebrity was not easy, Beyoncé learned. The constant touring and rehearsing, as well as the personal drama the group went through, were tiring for her. While she made it clear that it was not easy being a star, she also noted that some sacrifices were necessary to make a dream come true. She realized that if she did not accept the difficulties that came with being a celebrity, she would not last long in the music business.

Jon Wiederhorn, "Beyoncé Knowles: Destiny's Child," *Teen Magazine*, March 2001, p. 56.

Lynn Norment, "Beyoncé Heats Up Hollywood!" *Ebony*, July 2002, p. 36.

Christopher John Farley, "Call of the Child," *Time*, January 15, 2001, p. 128.

chances to shine and that she produced songs for the others to sing lead vocals on.

Beyoncé said Roberson and Luckett no longer had the same view of the group she and Rowland did. Once success entered the picture, the group members began to compete for attention and were looking out for themselves rather than doing what was best for the group as a whole. "Once you get money involved in anything, it gets crazier," Beyoncé says. "In the beginning, when we were all so ambitious and shared the same dream of becoming big stars, it was much easier to get along."[22]

The unhappiness within the group lasted for a year. Beyoncé said she and Rowland tried to resolve their differences with Roberson and Luckett. They spoke about the issues with their youth pastor, and when the group was on the road, the girls took turns sharing rooms. Despite these efforts, however, the rifts between the group members became too deep to bridge. On December 14, 1999, Luckett and Roberson sent identical letters to the group announcing that they no longer wanted Mathew Knowles to manage their careers. They felt he was playing up his daughter's talents at their expense.

Although they had known Luckett and Roberson had not been happy with the way things were going, Beyoncé, Rowland, and Beyoncé's parents were stunned when they received the letters. "We had never heard anything about them wanting another manager until we got the letters," Beyoncé says. "At first we were thinking, 'Well maybe they should get their own manager and we should try to work it out.' But you can't have two managers."[23]

Taking It Personally

In a lawsuit the two former group members eventually filed against Destiny's Child, they accused Mathew Knowles of "greed, insistence on control, self-dealing, and promotion of his daughter's interests at [their] expense."[24] Knowles defended his actions, noting that the girls were young when he became their manager, and he needed to have control of the group. He also noted that he and

LaToya Luckett (pictured) and LaTavia Roberson left Destiny's Child because they no longer wanted Mathew Knowles to manage their careers.

Tina had sold their house in order to finance the group, and said the group owed him thousands of dollars. The lawsuit was ultimately settled out of court.

Although she was eventually able to put the group's split behind her, Beyoncé initially took the move by Luckett and Roberson personally. She was hurt that her onetime friends had left the group so bitterly and publicly, and she compared the experience to breaking up with a boyfriend. She was also hurt by criticism from the public and magazine articles that cast her as a prima donna who monopolized the microphone. "Up to then I had never had anything bad happen to me, and it really threw me because I became the villain and that hurt so bad," she says. "I was only about 17 or 18, and all of a sudden I'm walking through airports and hearing people say, 'I can't stand her, she just thinks she's all that.' And I wanted so badly to say, 'You don't even know me. How can you judge me?'"[25]

The situation was so painful for Beyoncé that all she wanted to do was hide. For a time, all she could do was stay in her room. "For a month I stayed in bed," she said. "I was sad, hurt, on the verge of a nervous breakdown. I was thinking. 'Is all this worth it?' But I realized it's dumb to dwell on negativity."[26]

Rowland, who was also stung by the breakup, credited Tina Knowles with helping her and Beyoncé understand that things would get better. "My Aunt Tina would come in the room and say, 'No, we're not going to sit around in a funk today,'" Rowland said. "'We're going to get out and be positive, and we're going to make this situation better.'"[27]

Plus Two

In addition to being hurt by the criticisms of Luckett and Roberson, Beyoncé was also concerned about what their departure meant for the future of the group. She had worked hard to make the group a success, and now it was falling apart just as the girls were achieving what they had set out to accomplish. She was unsure whether Destiny's Child could survive with the loss of half of its members.

Farrah Franklin and Michelle Williams (second and third from left) joined Destiny's Child in 2000.

Knowles, however, had no doubt that Destiny's Child would endure. He soon began auditioning singers to replace Roberson and Luckett. Haste was necessary because Destiny's Child was slated to make a video for the song "Say My Name" a few weeks after Luckett and Roberson announced they no longer wanted Knowles to manage them. If the video was to be shot on schedule, the group needed to have two new members by the time filming began. "Either Destiny's Child would self-destruct, or we would find two new members,"[28] Beyoncé said.

After the auditions, experienced performers Michelle Williams and Farrah Franklin were added to the group. Williams had been a backup singer for the rhythm-and-blues artist Monica, and Franklin had been a dancer in the "Bills, Bills, Bills" video for Destiny's Child. The new members would be in the video for the song "Say My Name," but because the song had been recorded

Destiny's Child wows their audience during the **VH1 Divas** *concert in New York.*

before they joined the group, Roberson and LaTavia's voices would be on the soundtrack. To help make this less obvious in the video, it was crowded with extra dancers, and Williams and Franklin lip-synched the words to the song. Beyoncé was nervous about fan reaction to the video, but the changes within the group made viewers watch it more closely as they tried to identify the two new members. The video stayed on MTV and *Total Request Live* for months, and the song went to number one.

The group worked extra hard as Williams and Franklin tried to learn dance numbers in time for planned performances, television appearances, and a world tour. They gave their first live performance during the NBA's All-Star weekend in February 2000, and although Beyoncé was worried about performing in front of the celebrities who were attending, the appearance went smoothly. The group also performed at the Soul Train Awards and appeared on the *VH1 Divas 2000* show with music legend Diana Ross. After all the problems the group had experienced, Beyoncé was elated and amazed to be singing next to such an established star. "It's like a roller coaster going up," Beyoncé said of her career. "I just pray it never drops."[29]

Minus One

The relationships within the group did not remain harmonious for long, however. The group had a long list of appearances and rehearsals planned, and Franklin balked at the rigorous practice and performance schedule. In the first half of 2000, Destiny's Child performed in Alaska, New York, and other states before leaving for performances in the Netherlands, Belgium, and Germany. The group then returned to the United States for several appearances and prepared to go on tour in Australia.

Franklin missed a number of publicity appearances, and when it came time to leave for Australia, she did not come to the airport, despite frantic phone calls from Beyoncé and other group members. After she refused to accompany them on the trip, Franklin was dropped from the group. "Basically we had five performances last year, and Farrah decided she wasn't going to

By this time a trio, Destiny's Child performs on **The Early Show** *in 2001.*

come to them," Beyoncé later said. "She said she needed some time off, but she wasn't sick. No one had died in her family. Nothing had happened."[30]

A Stable Trio

Beyoncé, Rowland, and Williams decided to go ahead with their planned shows in Australia without Franklin. They quickly adapted their dance numbers for a trio rather than a quartet, and Beyoncé found the resulting show even better than the previous one that had included Franklin. "The show was tighter and, frankly, it looked better, too—we were all about the same height and there was a great vibe," Beyoncé said. "Not a trace of negativity."[31]

After successful shows in Australia, Beyoncé, Rowland, and Williams decided to remain a trio. There was no longer dissension within the group, which Beyoncé found refreshing. The women could finally concentrate on their music and enjoy their performances without worrying about hurting someone's feelings. Still, Beyoncé and the others were concerned about how the public would react. "We were all real nervous," Williams says. "The girls were like, 'Okay, what are we about to go through again?'"[32]

Defending Themselves

The girls braced themselves for negative reactions and snide comments about the group's revolving door, but Williams defended Beyoncé. "The group is not what people think it is," she said. "Beyoncé and Kelly are not what people think. They say Kelly is just riding the coattail of Beyoncé and Beyoncé is hogging everything. Beyoncé has God-given talent. It's just plain. It's not about her father managing the group. She's a great writer and producer."[33]

There was no denying that the entire Knowles family was involved in the group. In addition to Mathew as the manager, Tina as the stylist, and Beyoncé as a songwriter and producer, Beyoncé's younger sister, Solange, was a backup singer. Tina and Mathew Knowles said they had not begun working with Destiny's Child to benefit themselves. They noted that they had given up stable careers to focus on making the group a success. "We gave it up to make our kids' dreams come true," Tina Knowles says. "It's not like we planned this so that we could get rich off our kids."[34]

Rather than being a hard-driving manager, Mathew Knowles said he was offering guidance to the girls. "I believe in setting goals and getting the job done, and having everybody understand that this is where we've got to go," he says. "If there are some issues that need to be addressed, then I'll put them on the table. They always know where I'm coming from."[35]

Good and Bad Side

Comments about the group's management and personnel changes once more gave Destiny's Child extra media attention, and it was again painful for Beyoncé to see the group's affairs play out in public. However, she also saw how the additional media coverage boosted sales of the group's CDs and tour tickets. "Destiny's Child was always very talented," Beyoncé says in a *Newsweek* article, "but I think the thing we were lacking was controversy. I think in order for your group to be successful your story has to be interesting. Our story was very squeaky clean, so I thank God for the controversy. I'm happy because it helps me sell records."[36]

Despite the turmoil, the group remained strong musically. At the Grammy Awards in February 2001, Destiny's Child was up for five awards. It was also slated to perform, and Beyoncé felt a great deal of pressure because the performance would take place in front of so many other talented musicians. She felt the audience would be expecting to see why the group deserved so many nominations, and when she spotted established performers such as Madonna in the front row, that pressure intensified. She wanted to prove to the musical stars that Destiny's Child was worthy of the credit it was receiving. "I'll never forget all of the people in the audience who were shooting us skeptical looks in the very beginning—they were like, 'What do y'all think you're doing up on that stage,'" she says. "But by the end of the performance everyone was on their feet clapping."[37]

Kelly Rowland, Beyoncé, and Michelle Williams (left to right) graciously accept their Grammy for best rhythm-and-blues song, "Say My Name."

The appeal of the group was confirmed with two Grammy wins, one for best rhythm-and-blues song for "Say My Name" and one for best rhythm-and-blues performance by a duo or group. Beyoncé also won the 2001 Songwriter of the Year award from the American Society of Composers, Authors, and Publishers (ASCAP). She was the first black woman, and second woman ever, to win the ASCAP award. Beyoncé felt Destiny's Child was carving its own niche in the music world. "Our style of music and our style in general is different than any other," she said. "We want to be in a class by ourselves. Fifty years from now we want young groups to say they want to be like Destiny's Child."[38]

Survivor

Building on its success, the trio continued to tour around the world, and Beyoncé kept writing songs. She wrote "Independent Women Part I," which was used on the *Charlie's Angels* sound-track, and also produced material for the group's next album, *Survivor*. The title for the album reflected all that the group had gone through in the past year and was inspired by a comment by a radio disc jockey. During an interview, he had jokingly said the group was like the television show *Survivor*, with members departing on a regular basis. Beyoncé thought the title was funny and fitting, so it became the name of the group's next album.

The dramatic turns of the past year added fire to Beyoncé's songwriting. She channeled the pain of the group's discord into her music. "It seems that the songs I write because of extreme anger, happiness, or sadness become the biggest hits," she said. "I guess that's because a lot of other people can relate to them. For me the studio is where I go to get stuff off my chest and melodies out of my head. It's my therapy."[39]

Beyoncé played a major role in the production of *Survivor*, which was released in May 2001, writing or producing each track. However, she was also more than happy to share the lead vocals on the album with Williams and Rowland. She was intent on keeping their friendship firm. "If you have only a working relationship with people in your group, I don't know how you can possibly survive,"[40] she says.

Nineteen-year-old Beyoncé also used *Survivor* to show that her life was not all fun and glamour. The songs "DC-3" and "Fancy" make references to the group's breakup, and in "Happy Face," Beyoncé sings about how she had to look happy even when she felt miserable. She also addresses the serious topic of sexual abuse in "Story of Beauty," and "Gospel Medley" highlights the group members' Christian faith. "Bootylicious" was her commentary that all body shapes should be acceptable. "I wrote that song because I was getting bigger and bigger and I just wanted to talk about it," she says. "I like to eat and that's a problem in this industry."[41]

The album also opened old wounds for the group. In the lawsuit settlement with Roberson and Luckett, everyone involved with Destiny's Child had agreed not to make unflattering comments about each other. Roberson and Luckett said the "Survivor"

Too Much Destiny's Child?

After *Survivor* hit the top of the charts as soon as it debuted, Destiny's Child began getting a great deal of media exposure. In addition to advertisements for the new album and the Total Request Live tour the group would headline, there was also the "Survivor" video on MTV and other shows about the group. Nineteen-year-old Beyoncé worried that the media push might lead to overexposure, fearing that if the group was not selective enough in what it did, its appeal would evaporate. "I just hope people don't get sick of us," she said. "I'm sick of us, and I'm in Destiny's Child. . . . There has to be some mystery so people are excited when they see you."

Quoted in Lorraine Ali, "A Date with Destiny," *Newsweek*, May 21, 2001, p. 54.

Their Own Destiny

One of the strengths of Destiny's Child was its ability to have control over the music it produced. Beyoncé cowrote most of the songs on *Survivor* and had a hand in producing all of its tracks. This control contributed to the group's success. "The fact is, creatively, they're in charge," said Don Ienner, who was president of Columbia Records. "This is not [the product of a] producer's vision. These girls are basically writing, producing, and conceptualizing what they're talking about."

Quoted in Rashaun Hall, "Destiny's Child Cast as 'Survivor,'" *Billboard*, May 5, 2001, p. 12.

lyrics "You thought I wouldn't sell without you, sold 9 million" violated that agreement. The issue was resolved quickly, however, and a few months after the lawsuit was filed, it was settled out of court.

The lawsuit did not hurt sales of *Survivor.* The album debuted at the top of the charts in May 2001 and sold more copies in a week than any other album by a female group of the previous ten years. Despite its commercial success, however, critics gave it mixed reviews. Reviewer David Browne noted in *Entertainment Weekly* that Beyoncé's control over the album's content had both good and bad results. "Some of *Survivor*'s tracks try too hard and, as a result, forfeit the breeziness of the best moments on their previous album," he wrote, adding that the album contained too many songs that had the girls patting each other on the back. However, he also added that the album had a number of strong songs and that Beyoncé remained appealing: "The trio's overly processed harmonies threaten to rob them of personality, but even their missteps seem very human; you want to root for them."[42]

Celebrity Status

Browne's review also commented on the group's transitions, and he speculated about Beyoncé leaving Destiny's Child to begin a solo career. Although the group was thriving and Beyoncé was careful to give her fellow singers credit and a chance to take the lead on some songs, she was now a star in her own right. The group's Grammy Awards only added to her celebrity. "The honors confirm Beyoncé's status—she has earned the right to go by a single name—as a major star,"[43] Christopher John Farley wrote in *Time* magazine.

Ironically, although the public drama of the group's changes had worn on Beyoncé, they had also helped her become more famous. Yet she did not waver in her loyalty to the group or in her friendship with Rowland and Williams. At the same time, however, she could not deny her talent or the attention she was getting. She was poised to become an even bigger star.

Chapter 4

Breaking into Acting

Although Beyoncé enjoyed performing with Destiny's Child, it was becoming more and more apparent that she had enough talent to take her beyond the group. She knew there were things she could do outside the trio, but she did not want to appear to be a diva who was cutting ties with a group that was holding her back. In order for her career to move forward, she would have to strike out on her own, but she wanted to make her exit a graceful one. She planned to stay on good terms with Rowland and Williams and work with them again.

Leaving Destiny's Child

Acting and a solo album were both possibilities for Beyoncé, but before she could pursue them she needed to find a way to leave Destiny's Child for a time. The solution was for the group to take a break from touring and recording but not officially to split up. The break would give Beyoncé and the other group members the chance to pursue other performing opportunities that had come their way. Beyoncé was not the only one moving on; Rowland and Williams also had solo projects in the works. With the group's status on hold, they were all free to pursue something different.

Carmen

Instead of staying with recording, songwriting, and dancing, Beyoncé next went in a different direction with her career. MTV executives who thought she might be right to play the lead role in the network's 2001 production of *Carmen: A Hip-Hopera* sent a representative to a Destiny's Child show to request that she take a look at the script. Beyoncé was surprised to be asked to take the part. She had never acted before, and the title character's devious personality was quite unlike her own. However, when the opportunity arose, she saw it as too promising a career move to

Beyoncé appears in a scene from MTV's movie Carmen: A Hip-Hopera, *her first starring role.*

Making Music

Beyoncé was not the only member of Destiny's Child who stayed busy during the break the group began in 2001. Rowland recorded the solo album *Simply Deep*, which featured "Dilemma," a duet with rap star Nelly. Williams made the gospel albums *Heart to Yours* and *Do You Know*.

pass up. The singing role would allow her to explore acting in a way that took advantage of her vocal talent. "I think music is something that can, and should, be used to get you into different things," she says, "because eventually what goes up must come down—we're not going to be the number one group in the world forever—so you have to have something else to fall back on."[44]

Going Solo

The role as Carmen gave Beyoncé the opportunity to extend her performing talent beyond music and allowed her to grow in other ways as well. While filming *Carmen* over a period of three months, she was away from her family and Rowland for the first time. She had to learn to rely on herself.

On her own, Beyoncé became stronger and more independent. Without the other group members by her side, she had to learn to deal with the press alone and assert herself in discussions with the director. "I had to talk to directors, learn how to communicate my concerns, and speak up for myself," she says. "Essentially, I grew up a lot, both as a woman and a businesswoman."[45]

Beyoncé also grew as a performer. Although she had no acting experience, once she got to the set of *Carmen*, Beyoncé learned she had been acting without realizing it. She had performed onstage and in Destiny's Child videos, and as a celebrity with an image to uphold, she could not always reveal her true emotions. She had learned to hide her feelings, never letting fans know when she was down or depressed. Thus, she had been unconsciously acting every time she appeared in public. "I guess one of the reasons I found the transition from singer to actress pretty easy is because when you are in the public eye like we are, you have to learn how to put on a show," she says. "Not only do we have to give a great performance onstage, but sometimes we have to perform offstage, too."[46]

Goldmember *stars Mike Myers and Beyoncé mug for the camera. Beyoncé played a 1970s-era secret agent in the movie.*

Foxxy Move

Beyoncé's performance in *Carmen* caught the attention of producer John Lyons, who was involved in the production of the movie *Austin Powers in Goldmember*, starring Mike Myers. Lyons thought Beyoncé would be the perfect person to play Foxxy Cleopatra, a 1970s-era secret agent. "I felt strongly she was our girl from the very beginning, because she lit up every frame of that project and that was just her first acting role," Lyons said. "She has this Streisand-like quality, where you just know she can do anything and have this amazing career in both music and film."[47]

Beyoncé was not so sure that another acting role was the best career move for her to make, however. She was insecure about her acting ability, and the role required more acting than singing. She also thought she might be seen as just another singer using her fame to get a movie part without having any real talent for acting. "I was scared because some singers who become actors get a lot of criticism,"[48] she said.

Presidential Performance

Destiny's Child performed at the inauguration of President George W. Bush, who is also from Texas, in January 2001. They said their performance was not politically motivated, but instead was aimed at the kids in the audience. "They really, really wanted us to do it, and he's our president," Beyoncé says. "He told us that we have a bigger influence on kids than he does a lot of the time, and he appreciates that we're positive role models."

Quoted in Lorraine Bracco, "Destiny's Child," *Interview*, August 2001, p. 84.

Despite her reservations, Beyoncé agreed to read with Mike Myers for the part. She did not think her initial audition as the sexy secret agent went well. She was nervous and admitted to the director she had never done comedy before. "I read with Mike and just tried to be the straight guy." she said. "When I left, I was convinced I wasn't going to get it."[49]

Lyons saw enough potential in Beyoncé's audition, however, to ask her to come back a second time. This time she put more effort into the tryout. To prepare, she watched so-called blaxploitation films of the 1970s, and when she arrived at the audition she was dressed for the role. Wearing a skintight catsuit and Afro wig, she looked the part of a 1970s secret agent in the world of Austin Powers. The outfit put her in the right frame of mind, and her second audition went much better. "She just came in and nailed it,"[50] Lyons said.

Support on the Set

Beyoncé had won the part, but she was still not confident that she would be able to carry it off. She was initially nervous on the set and admitted that memorizing lines was not easy for her. However, costar Mike Myers defends her professionalism. "She came to the set prepared in every way, every day," he says. "In fact, she was overprepared."[51]

Beyoncé did not try to hide her inexperience from the rest of the cast, and the others did their best to make her feel comfortable. She was quiet while she was on the set, as the introverted side of her personality took over, until it came time for her to appear before the camera. Then she put on the glamorous bravado of Foxxy Cleopatra, the lead singer of a group of girls at a roller disco.

The onscreen result was a feminine but determined spy. Reviewer Lisa Schwarzbaum in *Entertainment Weekly* said her sweet and sexy take on an undercover agent worked well in the film. "Beyoncé Knowles, comely third of the best-selling girl group Destiny's Child, is far softer in her feature-film acting debut as Foxxy than the original Afro chicks, but Knowles' sweetness plays

Beyoncé poses for the paparazzi at the Goldmember premier in 2002. The movie was a box-office success.

nicely against the badass swagger of her talk and the fabulous-
ness of her wardrobe and 'dos,"[52] Schwarzbaum wrote.

Handling the Pressure

With her successful turn in *Goldmember*, Beyoncé had overcome
another career hurdle. She had a solid reputation as a singer, producer, and dancer, and she was gaining credit for her acting ability as well. However, while she portrayed an independent, strong
woman onstage and on-screen, offstage the twenty-year-old admitted that it was not always easy to handle the pressure. "It's overwhelming sometimes," she said. "I'm happy, but at the same time.
I'm not sure how long I want to do this. You have a lot to worry
about all the time."[53]

Beyoncé was not new to responsibility. She acknowledged that
she had not had much time to be a carefree teenager. Busy building a career, she had learned at a young age how to handle the
demands of her full schedule. "I've had the responsibility since I
was fifteen of someone who is twenty-five or thirty, so now I have

Beautiful and Humble

In 2001, *People* named Beyoncé one of the fifty most beautiful people in the world. However, the singer was not cer-
tain she belonged on the list. She noted that when she was
younger, she used to get teased about having large ears, and
she still saw flaws in herself every day. She wished for more
muscular legs and a smaller waist. "I have many insecurities,"
she said. "I think they keep you humble."

Beyoncé Knowles, (The 50 Most Beautiful People in the World 2001), *People*, May 14,
2001, p. 152.

a lot of pressure," she said. "I employ a lot of people, I make a lot of adult decisions, and that has forced me to grow up a little faster."[54]

Her increasing celebrity brought about a new challenge for the performer. Finding a balance between the demands of fame and her need for some privacy became more difficult as her popularity grew. Beyoncé knew that to succeed as a performer, she had to do interviews and have her famous face in magazines, but at the same time she did not want to give up the ability to venture out in public without being bothered. While on tour with Destiny's Child, she had vacationed in Thailand and enjoyed the pleasure of walking down the beach without having anyone know who she was.

Such private times became rarer and rarer, however, as she became more of a public figure. It was difficult for her to go unrecognized in public, and Beyoncé tried hard to show the humble, gracious side of her personality to her fans. When one fan approached her for an autograph while she was on the phone with her family, crying because an uncle had died, she did not resent the intrusion. "If I was like, 'I can't talk to you right now,' she might never see me again. I can't do that," Beyoncé says. "That fan wouldn't understand it. You've got to put it off and sign that autograph. It's hard, don't get me wrong, but it's something I've got to do."[55]

While the pressure of upholding a positive image and doing all that a busy career demanded was not always easy for her to handle, Beyoncé did not want people to feel sorry for her. She was doing what she loved. She acknowledged that there had been bad times as well as good in her life, but she said her life had not been unhappy and she was fortunate to have had the success that had come her way. "You have to know that you're blessed and that it's not all about you," she says. "You have to know that yeah, you might be talented, you might work hard, but it can all be taken away. There are a million other girls my age that are as talented—if not more talented—as I am. Whatever I've got, they've got more of. So I'm lucky that I'm able to do this."[56]

With Jay-Z, Privately

One way Beyoncé tried to protect her privacy was to avoid revealing more about her personal life than was necessary. This was

Jay-Z and Beyoncé met in 2000 when they recorded a duet for one of his albums.

especially true when she began dating rapper Jay-Z, whose given name is Shawn Corey Carter. Photos of the two together were published, but even then Beyoncé hesitated to call him her boyfriend. "We're good friends,"[57] she told a reporter with a smile.

The two had worked together in November 2000 when they had released the duet "Bonnie and Clyde," the first single off Jay-Z's album *Blueprint II: The Gift and the Curse.* They seemed an unlikely pair. He was eleven years older than she was and a rapper. Beyoncé had a much softer musical style. However, their dedication to the music business and their talent gave them much in common.

Time to Herself

Up to this point in her career, Beyoncé had not had a great deal of time to invest in developing a relationship. Now, however, she took the opportunity to relax while Destiny's Child was on break. Like the other members of the group, Beyoncé had been set to release a solo album in late 2002. However, she decided to delay the album while she took some time off.

Soon, however, she began to look forward to completing her solo album and reuniting with Destiny's Child to close that chapter of her life before continuing on her own. She was preparing to wind down her time with the group in a positive way, and then focus on her career as a solo artist and actress.

Chapter 5

Solo Sensation

Beyoncé's acting roles demonstrated that she was ready and able to stand on her own as a solo performer. She looked for new acting parts and as a singer was eager to take on a solo role as well. She readied her own album and developed a hip-shaking signature dance move, raising her level of recognition another notch.

Success as a solo singer and actress proved that Beyoncé was popular enough to advance her career without Destiny's Child. However, she remained loyal to the group that had launched her to stardom. The group began making another album, as they had promised their fans they would. In addition to showing that she was a person who kept her word, the Destiny's Child reunion was also a retreat to a comfortable role for Beyoncé. She had been trying many new things on her own, and it was reassuring to have her friends waiting for her to return. She knew her time with the group would have to end someday, but for now she looked forward to working with her friends again.

The Fighting Temptations

After the success of *Goldmember*, Beyoncé's acting career continued with *The Fighting Temptations*. This comedy starred Cuba Gooding Jr. as a man who must form a successful gospel choir before he can collect an inheritance. Beyoncé played an unwed mother singing in a jazz club. The role gave her the opportunity to try something new both in acting and in music. "The great thing is that I'm doing music that I wouldn't normally do as Beyoncé or Destiny's Child," she said. "I'm doing serious old-school hymns, and I get to do some really soulful, funky stuff."[58]

Thanks to Mom

Even as she became a bigger and bigger star, Beyoncé looked homeward to her mother for inspiration. She credited her mother with helping her achieve her dream. From her mother, Beyoncé inherited a sense of style and learned other things as well. "I've learned lots of important things from my mama," she says. "However, there are two lessons that stand out in my mind: One is, outer beauty means nothing because it fades; and everything you do in the dark will one day come to light."

Tina Knowles (left) has always been a big inspiration for her daughter.

Quoted in *Ebony*, "Serena and Venus on the Fabulous Oracene, Mother of the Williams Dynasty," May 2003, p. 156.

Beyoncé encourages others to sing in this scene from **The Fighting Temptations.**

While the movie gave her the opportunity to expand her musical repertoire, it did little to advance her acting career. The movie attracted scant attention when it was released in the summer of 2003, and Beyoncé's performance received lukewarm reviews. Reviewer Leah Rozen said Beyoncé's acting was short on substance and her singing lacked a powerful signature tune. "As a small-town honey wise to the city slicker's lines, Knowles is gorgeous but mistakes attitude for acting," Rozen wrote. "Not surprisingly, the pop diva is most effective when singing, though the film never gives her a tune with which to blow the roof off, which is what viewers keep hoping for and *Temptations* sorely needs."[59]

Dangerously in Love

Beyoncé had a much more enthusiastic reception for her solo album, *Dangerously in Love*, which was also released in 2003. She showed a variety of musical styles on the CD, which included hip-hop dance tracks, soothing ballads, and songs with a rhythm-and-blues feel. The first song on the CD, "Crazy in Love," began with a burst of trumpets and had an infectious "uh-oh" in the chorus. In the slower-paced "Daddy," she paid tribute to her father and all he had done for her. A number of other popular musicians contributed to her effort, including Missy Elliot, Sean Paul, Mario Winans, Big Boi, and Luther Vandross. However, Beyoncé again took charge of the production and wrote many of the album's songs.

Beyoncé's boyfriend Jay-Z also contributed to the album by putting the finishing touches on its first hit single, "Crazy in Love." Beyoncé wrote the song but initially struggled with it because she had extremely high expectations for it. She had written number-one songs for Destiny's Child and expected nothing less from a song she would write for herself alone.

Yet she felt her first draft of "Crazy in Love" was mediocre. Something was lacking, but she was not sure what it was. From her experience with Destiny's Child, she knew the song needed to have something special if it was to become a hit. She thought perhaps having a rapper contribute to it would make the difference, and Jay-Z was happy to oblige. The night before Beyoncé was due to finish the song, he came into the studio at 3 a.m. He listened to the song for a few minutes, mouthed a few words, and then came out with a rap that he mixed with traditional lyrics to give the song exactly the edge it needed. "He rapped on the song and he added a lot to the energy of it," Beyoncé says. "It really completed the song."[60]

Being Herself

Beyoncé wrote and produced other songs for *Dangerously in Love* as well, and for the first time, she felt she could truly express herself with her music. She did not need to worry about being too selfish with the lyrics or not sharing enough of the songs. Because she was not concerned about upstaging anyone, she did not feel she had to limit her talents and could show off a range of styles. "I can sing like a rapper, I can flow, I can sing soul songs, I can do rock, and I wanted people to hear that,"

Jay-Z and Beyoncé perform a song from her first solo album,
Dangerously in Love, *at the 2003 MTV Video Music Awards.*

she says. "All the Destiny's Child songs like 'Independent Woman' and 'Survivor' were all so strong. I wanted people to hear the more vulnerable side."[61]

The album quickly went platinum and yielded a number of singles, including "Me, Myself and I," "Baby Boy," and "Naughty Girl." It earned her five Grammy Awards as well as positive comments from critics. Reviewer Neil Drumming gave the CD an A-minus and praised the chances Beyoncé took with the album. "*Dangerously in Love*, her solo debut, confirms her taste for innovation," he said. "The results are not half bad—certainly not the first half."[62] Drumming praised "Crazy in Love," with its big horn intro and catchy refrain; "Naughty Girl;" and "Baby Boy." While not all of the songs sounded as innovative as these, he gave Beyoncé credit for trying something new. Beyoncé promoted the album with a European tour and taped a concert in London that was made into the *Live at Wembley* DVD.

Signature Dance

Beyoncé also received recognition for a signature dance she did in the video for "Crazy in Love." She had been looking for a move that people would associate with her and only her, something they would watch for when she was onstage. To accomplish this, a choreographer helped her develop a rapid hip-shaking move.

Although it had been something she had set out to do, Beyoncé was surprised how thoroughly the move became connected with her. She was asked to do it when she was interviewed on television, and talk show host Oprah Winfrey even asked Beyoncé to teach her how to do it. The dance helped Beyoncé earn MTV Video Music Awards in 2003 for best rhythm-and-blues video and best choreography.

Beyoncé's reputation as a solo artist grew as she headlined a solo tour with Missy Elliot and Alicia Keys in 2004. This Ladies First tour was her first sold-out tour as a solo artist. She did not perform completely alone, however. Jay-Z appeared with her during the concerts to sing their hit "Crazy in Love." Their relationship was slowly moving into the spotlight, and Beyoncé

Mom's Approval

Beyoncé did not speak publicly about her relationship with rapper Jay-Z, although they performed together, were photographed together in public, and were clearly a couple. Beyoncé's mother approved of their relationship, saying that Jay-Z was a good match for her daughter. "Jay is just such a gentleman, and he is so smart," Tina Knowles says, "I was so happy that they got together. They're two smart people, and it's great for both of them."

Quoted in Lisa Robinson, "Above and Beyoncé," *Vanity Fair*, November 2005, p. 336.

acknowledged it in public when she mentioned him during the 2004 MTV Video Music Awards. However, even though they were photographed together, she still refused to talk about him with the press.

Sasha

While Beyoncé continued to keep her personal life as private as possible, onstage she became even more uninhibited. During her tour as a solo artist, she took her dancing to another level. As a member of Destiny's Child, Beyoncé had to perform in a way that blended in with the other group members, holding back so she would not dominate the group's performance. "I always held back in Destiny's Child, because I was comfortable in a group and felt that I didn't have to do anything 100 percent, because there were other people onstage with me," she says. "I would not lose myself or go all the way."[63]

Yet as a solo act, Beyoncé could no longer rely on the other members of the group to take the spotlight. She needed to have

Beyoncé puts on a stunning performance in Las Vegas in 2004.

moves that were strong enough to carry her performance. All eyes were focused on her, and she could feel free to do all she wanted to entertain the audience.

Ever since Beyoncé had been a child, she had found that her personality changed when she was onstage. That feeling intensified when she became a solo artist. She developed an onstage alter ego she called Sasha to express how she felt like a different person when she was performing. Offstage, she was still quiet and introverted, but onstage she was not afraid to do anything. She explains:

> I don't have a split personality, but I'm really very country and would rather have no shoes on and have my hair in a bun and no makeup. And when I perform this confidence and this sexiness and whatever it is that I'm completely not just happens. And you feel it and you just start wildin' and doin' stuff that don't even make sense, like the spirit takes over.[64]

It took more than sexy dances to be a successful performer, however. Her years of rehearsing and performing experience also gave Beyoncé onstage poise. She did not get flustered if things did not go exactly as planned. During the 2004 Academy Awards telecast, Beyoncé was slated to sing three songs. When it came time for her to sing "Learn to Be Lonely" from *Phantom of the Opera*, she realized her high-heeled shoe was not snapped and her ear monitor was not on. She had to walk down a set of stairs, and she could not tell if she was in time to the music or not. Worse, her unsnapped shoe got stuck in the bottom of her long dress. Despite the miscues, however, she managed to balance on tiptoe, focus on singing the song, and make it look like nothing was wrong.

Cultivating an Image

While the sexy, onstage Sasha is very different from the real Beyoncé, the poise that she has as a performer carries over into her personal life. She is shy, but she also knows how to make people around her feel comfortable. "She's the beautiful girl in school who's disarmingly down to earth."[65] notes writer Toure in an article for *Rolling Stone*.

Although Beyoncé has cultivated an unrestrained image while she is performing, she presents a controlled one in public. She does not want to let fans see her lose control or act self-centered. To do this, she has learned to rein in her emotions. When her luggage was lost in Paris after a long trip from New Jersey to

France, for example, she appeared to a reporter to be annoyed but remained polite and professional.

Beyoncé is also open about her Christian faith and does not see it as conflicting with her stage personality. The Destiny's Child autobiography, *Soul Survivors*, contains some of her favorite Bible verses, and she unhesitatingly discusses her faith during interviews. Some of her costumes are revealing and her dances sexy, but she does not see this as being contradictory to her beliefs. "What's more important to me is the way I treat people, what I think, what I give to other people,"[66] she says.

The singer is careful to treat other people with kindness. While on tour, she tries to keep her requests low-key, asking for simple things such as cherry Jell-O gelatin, grapes, and diet Snapple tea. She does not want to be seen as a demanding, self-centered diva who makes outrageous requests.

Together Again

Loyalty is another trait of Beyoncé's, and as promised, she reunited with Rowland and Williams in June 2004 to record the final

Tiny Treat

Beyoncé had the determination to become a star and the willpower to keep herself looking her best. Although she has a sweet tooth, she indulges it by limiting herself to just a taste of the foods she craves. When she was at a Grammy party in February 2004, a plate of desserts was brought to her table. Beyoncé ate only a tiny slice of a chocolate brownie. "If you cut little slices it's not so bad," she told a reporter.

Quoted in Lisa Robinson, "Above and Beyoncé," *Vanity Fair*, November 2005, p. 336.

Destiny's Child shares a laugh with the host of MTV's TRL while promoting their final album, **Destiny Fulfilled.**

album for Destiny's Child. She wrote and produced many of the songs on *Destiny Fulfilled*, which was released in November 2004. Rowland and Williams sang lead vocals on many of the songs, as Beyoncé was ready to share the spotlight once again.

The album was a surprise to some who thought the solo projects done by the group members would be the end of Destiny's Child, but Beyoncé says the time apart was a period of professional development for all three women. "It was important for us to do our own things, so that we'd have the opportunity to grow and see what we could do on our own," she says. "It's really beautiful to do that and then also have the opportunity to come back together and have the fun we have when we are together. When you have that sort of friendship, recording doesn't feel like work."[67]

The album received mixed reviews. Reviewer Chuck Arnold of *People* noted that "*Destiny Fulfilled* . . . mostly picks up where the second two-thirds of Beyoncé's *Dangerously in Love* left off, with lots of luxurious slow-to-midtempo grooves that show off the trio's sexier, more supple vocals."[68]

Not every reviewer agreed with his assessment, however. "*Destiny Fulfilled* . . . often moves at a molasses-like pace, weighted down with a preponderance of exquisitely executed but ultimately dull ballads,"[69] wrote reviewer Tom Sinclair of *Entertainment Weekly*, who gave the album a C-plus.

Despite some negative reviews, the album was a commercial success. It made it to the top of *Billboard's* R&B/Hip-Hop chart and number two on the *Billboard 200*. Its singles included the uptempo "Lose My Breath" and "Soldier." Destiny's Child had proved once again that they could capture an audience.

Planning a Happy Ending

While Beyoncé enjoyed performing with Destiny's Child, she did not envision staying with the group much longer. She also could not see herself performing forever as a solo act. She expected one day to cut back on her hectic lifestyle and have a family. Ultimately, she looked forward to retiring early and enjoying what she had accomplished. "One day I wanna have a family and be a mother and occasionally put out albums or do like Anita Baker and perform occasionally,"[70] she says.

That day was still far off, however, as Destiny's Child prepared to promote its latest album. The upcoming tour would gracefully end Beyoncé's involvement in Destiny's Child. Afterward, she would be free to embark on new projects that would take advantage of her ever-increasing fame.

Chapter 6

Following Her Destiny

Even though she still loved performing with Rowland and Williams, Beyoncé continued to dedicate herself to broadening her career. She had the stage presence to be a solo act, and it was clearly time for her to leave Destiny's Child. She was a businesswoman as well as a performer and realized that while having Rowland and Williams onstage to support her was comforting, it was not helping her career.

Beyoncé was a businesswoman in other ventures as well. She took advantage of her celebrity status to release her own perfume. The careful management of her offstage image and her popular songs and dance moves gave her a name that sold products. By now, she was no longer just a singer, she was a figure that others wanted to emulate. This gave her the leverage to turn her name into a product.

The singer also planned to release another album, but she saw greater potential for career reward in acting. She was realizing that she could let herself go with an acting role, just as she had learned to do onstage. She decided that bigger roles and bigger pictures would be the next challenge for her to overcome.

The Pink Panther

Beyoncé's next opportunity for acting came in the summer of 2004 when she was approached with the offer of appearing in the movie *The Pink Panther* with Steve Martin and Kevin Kline. She had been

Beyoncé starred with comedian Steve Martin (right) in **The Pink Panther.**

writing songs for the new Destiny's Child album, but found herself with several weeks of free time. Rather than go on vacation, she decided to fill the time by taking the movie role.

The role seemed like a good career move for her. Filming would take only a few weeks, and she was happy to have the chance to work with well-known comic actor Martin. The role also allowed her to put her musical ability to use, as she wrote and performed a song for the movie's soundtrack.

Beyoncé had a good time on the set, but the film did not do much to advance her career as an actress other than showing that she was willing to work. Its release was delayed until early 2006, and it opened to poor reviews. "The French have a word for it," wrote reviewer Leah Rozen of *The Pink Panther*, "ooh-la-lame."[71] Reviewer Lisa Schwarzbaum noted in *Entertainment Weekly* that Beyoncé was likely cast in the movie to appeal to a younger audience but that she was the wrong choice for the role.

Destiny Fulfilled

The movie was a minor sidetrack in Beyoncé's career, however. Before it was released, she wrapped up her performances with Destiny's Child. To promote their *Destiny Fulfilled* album, the women went on a final tour. It was an extravagant show, requiring thirteen buses to carry all the dancers, caterers, and other staff members.

On the tour, Beyoncé showed how much she had matured as a businesswoman. Besides performing as a singer and dancer, she managed many details as well. When someone had a question, Beyoncé was the go-to person. "Beyoncé is undoubtedly Queen Bee, if for no other reason than her talent, vision and attention to the smallest detail," writes Jeannine Amber in *Essence* magazine. The writer added that Beyoncé did not take advantage of her authority and showed the poise that marked her offstage presence.

Destiny's Child performs in Tokyo, Japan, during their final tour in 2005.

"She's a benevolent ruler, her ambition tempered by compassion, her discipline softened by humor,"[72] Amber writes.

The tour took the group around the world, and wherever they were, Beyoncé felt obliged to keep things under control. When a fight broke out in an audience in Dubai over a towel the group had thrown into the audience, Beyoncé scolded the crowd. She also kept those close to her focused. Shortly before the tour started in Japan, Beyoncé's mother became upset with how one of Beyoncé's dresses for the show looked. Tina Knowles had searched Tokyo for the right material and spent two days and nights remaking the dress. When Beyoncé put it on and her mother hated how it looked, her mom was so upset that she started to cry. Beyoncé, however, was unfazed. "Beyoncé looked at me and said, 'Mom, I know you're sad, but you gotta pull it together,'" Knowles recalls. "'We have a show to do.'" Knowles adds, "Beyoncé's always like that. Just calm. She's always the center of calm."[73]

The End for Destiny's Child

The group members knew from the beginning that this would be their final tour, but they did not make an official announcement until July. While they were in Spain, they announced that the group would officially dissolve after the tour. "After a lot of discussion and some deep soul-searching, we realized that our current tour has given us the opportunity to leave Destiny's Child on a high note, united in our friendship and filled with overwhelming gratitude of our music, our fans, and each other,"[74] the group's statement announced.

Beyoncé, Rowland, and Williams noted that their years of working together had been wonderful, but they had all reached the point where it was best to pursue personal goals and solo efforts. They made it clear that the group was not breaking apart because of dissension among its members, but because it was time for a change for all of them. "This is a time of natural growth for all of us,"[75] the group's statement said.

The announcement caused more of a stir than Beyoncé and the other members of the group expected. It was carried in newspapers and was on CNN's newscasts. Since it had long been their

Music Master

The musical history lesson Beyoncé received from her parents when she was young paid off when she became a star. She impressed people, including her boyfriend Jay-Z, with her knowledge of music and her ability to sing along with songs such as Carlos Santana's "Oye Como Va" and "Across the Universe" by the Beatles. "It's crazy," Jay-Z says. "She's a student of the game. She's a student of all types of music. The sounds she can hear in music and memorize off one listen are amazing. She has a wonderful ear for music—knows if people are flat, on pitch, on tone—she has the whole thing down pat."

Quoted in Lisa Robinson, "Above and Beyoncé," *Vanity Fair*, November 2005, p. 336.

intention to go their separate ways after the tour, Beyoncé was surprised by the attention it received. "We've been saying the entire time that this last album was going to be the final album," she said. "That's why we called it *Destiny Fulfilled*. I didn't think it was like breaking news."[76]

Family Togetherness

After the announcement was made, the tour continued for several more months. The hectic, tiring schedule was made a little easier for Beyoncé because members of her extended family were able to accompany her. Her mother, sister, and her sister's baby son were with her during part of the European leg of the tour in the summer of 2005. Her cousin Angie was her personal assistant, and her cousin Marion was her road manager.

One person not present on the tour was Beyoncé's father. Mathew Knowles was still the group's manager, but as the group members had grown up, he had traveled with them less and less, staying behind to take care of business matters. Tina Knowles had done more traveling with the girls, because she was in charge of their costumes and hair. Beyoncé pushed aside rumors that her father had stayed away from the group after being accused of harassing one of the dancers. "My father is still our manager," she said. "He hasn't toured with us since we were 17. And he only did that because we couldn't afford a soundman, so he was doing sound."[77] Beyoncé had grown as a performer and business-woman to the point that she could take control on the road without her father's help.

An Evolving Relationship

Beyoncé had an evolving relationship with her parents. She had depended greatly on her father's guidance when she was a child and young teen, but she took more and more control of her career as she got older, writing songs and producing her own albums. It was not easy for her father to see his eldest daughter as an independent woman. However, he could not deny that Beyoncé was becoming less reliant on him and his guidance as she got older. She now had her own home and took care of many of the group's touring details on the road. She still respected her parents, but she did not need their advice as much as she had in the past. Beyoncé's relationship with her father was respectful, and her relationship with her mother was turning into friendship. "The older I get, the more we become friends,"[78] Beyoncé says.

Final Concert

Beyoncé said good-bye to her friends in Destiny's Child in 2005. The group gave its final concert on September 10. The members could not help becoming tearful as they looked at the audience and realized it would be the last time they would be performing together for the foreseeable future.

The concert marked the end of a chapter in their lives, but they were leaving as a success. In October, the group released the album

Fans get a final good-bye wave from Destiny's Child after a concert in Vancouver, British Columbia.

#1s, a compilation of the group's top-ranked hits, and it went to the top of the *Billboard* 200 chart. The group maintained a solid fan base, winning numerous awards and selling more than 40 million records worldwide. In addition, the three members of the group remained close friends who enjoyed working together. "We love each other and we love singing together," Beyoncé said. "This is not one of those situations where there's a bad ending because something crazy happened."[79]

Beyoncé did not discount the possibility that they would one day sing together again, although not for a major tour or another album. They could help out on each other's solo recordings or briefly reunite for a special event. Their careers would be taking them in new directions, but their friendship would remain stable. "Breakup sounds so final," Beyoncé says. "It's more like a growing up."[80]

Beyoncé (second from right) and modeling staff members look at images of her clothing line during a photo shoot.

Businesswoman

Beyoncé had indeed grown in her career. Her work with Destiny's Child had become only a fraction of all she did. She used her image to sell products as well as music, promoting Pepsi Cola, L'Oreal hair products, and her own fragrance, True Star. In January 2005, Beyoncé and her mother signed a licensing agreement with the Tarrant Apparel Group for a clothing line called the House of Dereon. Named after Beyoncé's seamstress grandmother, Agnes Dereon, the line included children's clothing.

Part of the reason for Beyoncé's commercial success was her wholesome image and good reputation. Companies did not have any qualms about having her represent them because she stayed out of trouble, worked hard, and continued to be successful. She had a stable rather than rocky relationship with her boyfriend Jay-Z, and was a mainstay on awards shows. She did not regularly appear in tabloids or gossip magazines. "Beyoncé—she of the 'bootylicious' sexy dances—still manages to wear her success well while maintaining a sense of decorum in a world gone absolutely mad. Beyoncé Knowles is very much a lady. And when was the last time anyone used that word to describe a superstar?"[81] wrote Lisa Robinson in a *Vanity Fair* article.

Onstage, Beyoncé did show a provocative side of her personality. However, that aspect of her character was for performances

Ignoring the Rumors

Even after she has achieved solo success and positive feedback as an actress, Beyoncé remains very aware of how she is portrayed on television and in print. She tries hard to project a clean image and do her best as a performer, but not every story written about her is complimentary. She has been in the business long enough to know not to release details of her private life but realizes that no matter how hard she tries, she can not control what is written about her. As a public figure, she is bound to be the subject of rumors and media interest. There have been reports that Beyoncé was firing her father to have Jay-Z manage her career, that her parents were splitting up, and that she was engaged or married.

It is still hurtful when things are said about her family, but over the years she has developed a strategy for coping with what is said. She tries hard to ignore negative comments and false rumors, because when she pays attention to them, they still sting. She has to brush them aside to save her sanity. "I don't have a choice," she says. "How else am I going to survive? If you're sensitive, it's gonna drive you crazy."

Quoted in Jeannine Amber, "Beyoncé's Destiny," *Essence*, October 2005, p. 158.

only. One writer compared her dance moves to those of a stripper, but also noted that she was quite a different person when she was not performing: "Offstage she carries herself with the modesty and reserve of a proper schoolgirl, acknowledging everyone from a driver to a fan with a soft-spoken appreciation, and impressing the public as an honest-to-God Real Nice Girl,"[82] Jeannine Amber wrote in *Essence* magazine.

Beyoncé may be flamboyant onstage, but when she is dancing for fun in public she does not use her sexy concert moves. At times she and Jay-Z did some salsa dancing when they were out together, but she did not show off her hip-shaking style. "People expect me to do that, but that's for the stage,"[83] she says.

She also continued to remain quiet about her personal relationships. While she and Jay-Z appeared together at professional basketball games, parties, and awards shows, she was still hesitant to speak in public about their relationship. "I never talked about my relationships," she says. "Even in school I never did. I only talk about them in my songwriting; otherwise things get too messy."[84]

Dream Role

The public's reaction to Beyoncé and her efforts in music and business has been for the most part positive, and her reputation as an actress also continues to grow. In 2005, she was offered a part in *Dreamgirls*, a movie based on a Broadway musical. The movie stars Jamie Foxx, Eddie Murphy, and Danny Glover, and it follows a fictional musical group over a fifteen-year period of time. Beyoncé was confident that this was the perfect role for her, as she knew she had the ability to do the singing and dancing required and she also liked the character. She thought the script was good and wanted the role badly, as she had been familiar with the musical for years. "I never wanted anything as much as I wanted that [part]," she says. "Finally, I am able to play a character with range."[85]

The role was broader than her previous acting jobs in *Austin Powers in Goldmember* and *The Fighting Temptations*. The movie would take months to shoot, as opposed to the three weeks she had spent on the set of *The Pink Panther*, and her part gave her

Jamie Foxx and Beyoncé celebrate their new film **Dreamgirls** *at the Cannes Film Festival in 2006.*

the type of acting challenge she was seeking. In *Dreamgirls*, she could finally show her skills as an actress. "I don't think people have any idea what I can do as an actor,"[86] she said.

Beyoncé wanted to become an actress who lost herself in the role, just as she lost herself in her performance when she sang and danced onstage. She wanted to take roles that challenged her to step into another person's thoughts and actions. Delivering an Oscar-winning performance one day is one of her goals, and she was confident that the right role would come her way. "What has to happen is like a tingling, something that happens where I can do anything, and I'm not scared—I'm just lost in the moment," she said. "I haven't done that with acting yet, but I know I can."[87]

Extra Effort, Rave Reviews

Knowing that the role in *Dreamgirls* was pivotal, Beyoncé prepared diligently for it. For two months before rehearsals began, she immersed herself in the music of the Supremes, the 1960s singing group that the musical is loosely based upon. She then spent two months in rehearsals for the movie.

Losing Herself

Beyoncé sometimes worried about losing her sense of self as she became more famous. She did not want the person she was deep inside to be overwhelmed by her celebrity. "I don't want to get addicted to fame," she says. "Then when I'm no longer famous I won't know what do to, and I'll just seem desperate and lose my mind." It was a struggle she had fought over the years, as she had been constantly busy. "You lose touch with who you are," she says. "When you work so much like we did, it's just too much."

Quoted in Toure, "A Woman Possessed," *Rolling Stone*, March 4, 2004, p. 38.

Beyoncé also challenged herself to change her look while making the movie and lost twenty pounds during filming. She wanted to show how her character changed as she got older, not just emotionally but physically as well. "I wanted it to be something more than just make-up and hair," she said. "I wanted to see the change."[88]

Audience members who got the first look at footage from *Dreamgirls* were impressed. A thirty-minute clip of the movie was shown at the Cannes Film Festival six months before it was due to be released in theaters, and the dazzled audience applauded and asked for more. Before the clips were shown, Beyoncé had told a reporter she was scared, but afterward she was so filled with relief and happiness that she cried. "I can't believe it,"[89] she said.

Inspiration

Making the movie inspired Beyoncé to finish her second solo album. She worked on it while filming *Dreamgirls* and recorded it in a few weeks. The album is filled with rhythm-and-blues songs influenced by the musical style in the movie. Beyoncé again had control over the album's material, as she and her father were the executive producers. She also had help from Rodney Jerkins and other songwriters and producers, and the first single from the album, "*Déjà Vu*," featured Jay-Z.

Called *B'day*, the album was set to be released internationally on Beyoncé's twenty-fifth birthday, September 4, 2006. Beyoncé promoted it with a tour and held open auditions for an all-girl band to back her up. The band was not another version of Destiny's Child, but a group of musicians who provided support for the popular singer.

Making a Difference

Beyoncé has kept her career moving at a brisk pace and is a well-known performer who continues to receive recognition for her work. In 2006, she and Stevie Wonder shared the Grammy Award for best rhythm-and-blues performance by a duo for the song "So Amazing." It was her ninth Grammy.

Beyoncé is clearly an established star, and while she continues to consider acting roles and release albums, she also wants to make an impact with her life beyond music and movies. She and the other members of Destiny's Child have opened a community center in Houston and have supported Ronald McDonald Houses while on tour. They have also helped find housing for some victims of 2005's Hurricane Katrina, who were forced to leave New Orleans.

Helping people is one of Beyoncé's goals. She is pleased when people tell her that her songs inspire them, and she enjoys being able to touch people with her music. However, she also wants to do something more tangible. She wants to leave a legacy that shows she is a caring person as well as a talented singer, dancer, and actress. "I want to take advantage of my celebrity to do something more than write songs that inspire people," she says. "Whether it's working with kids or going to Africa every year to raise awareness, or maybe just becoming a mother—I want to make my mark."[90]

Chapter 1: Groomed for Success

1. Quoted in Olivia Abel, "Chatter," *People*, August 5, 2002, p. 112.
2. Beyoncé Knowles, Kelly Rowland, Michelle Williams, and James Patrick Herman, *Soul Survivors: The Official Autobiography of Destiny's Child*. New York: HarperCollins, 2002, p. 10.
3. Quoted in Lisa Robinson. "Above and Beyoncé," *Vanity Fair*, November 2005, p. 336.
4. Quoted in Robinson, "Above and Beyoncé," p. 336.
5. Knowles et al., *Soul Survivors*, p. 54.
6. Quoted in Rob Brunner, "Someday We'll Be Together," *Entertainment Weekly*, September 1, 2000, p. 42.
7. Knowles et al., *Soul Survivors*, p. 58.
8. Quoted in Robinson, "Above and Beyoncé," p. 336.
9. Quoted in Robinson, "Above and Beyoncé," p. 336.
10. Quoted in Robinson, "Above and Beyoncé," p. 336.
11. Knowles et al., *Soul Survivors*, p. 10.
12. Knowles et al., *Soul Survivors*, p. 80.

Chapter 2: Child's Play

13. Quoted in Brunner, "Someday We'll Be Together," p. 42.
14. Quoted in Brunner, "Someday We'll Be Together," p. 42.
15. Knowles et al., *Soul Survivors*, p. 81.
16. Knowles et al., *Soul Survivors*, p. 85.
17. Knowles et al., *Soul Survivors*, p. 87.
18. Quoted in Evelyn McDonnell, "Destiny's Child," *Interview*, May 2000, p. 72.
19. Quoted in *Jet*, "Destiny's Child: Hot Young Divas Continue to Burn Up Music Charts," May 29, 2000, p. 58.
20. Quoted in *Cosmopolitan*, "Beyoncé Knowles: Dynamic Diva," February 1, 2002, p. 160.

21. Jeff Salamon, "Destiny's Child: The Writing's on the Wall," *Texas Monthly*, September 1999, p. 36.

Chapter 3: A New Destiny's Child

22. Knowles et al., *Soul Survivors*, p. 96.
23. Quoted in Brunner, "Someday We'll Be Together," p. 42.
24. Quoted in Brunner, "Someday We'll Be Together," p. 42.
25. Quoted in Allison Samuels, "What Beyoncé Wants," *Newsweek*, July 29, 2002, p. 52.
26. Quoted in Danyel Smith, "Meeting Their Destiny," *Teen People*, March 1, 2001, p. 104.
27. Quoted in Lorraine Bracco, "Destiny's Child," *Interview*, August 2001, p. 84.
28. Quoted in Christopher John Farley, "Call of the Child," *Time*, January 15, 2001, p. 128.
29. Quoted in *People*, "Four Fates," June 19, 2000, p. 82.
30. Quoted in Jon Wiederhorn, "Beyoncé Knowles: Destiny's Child," *Teen Magazine*, March 2001, p. 56.
31. Knowles et al., *Soul Survivors*, p. 5.
32. Quoted in Margena A. Christian, "Destiny's Child: Hot, Sexy Singing Group Soars to the Top," *Jet*, May 14, 2001, p. 56.
33. Quoted in Christian, "Destiny's Child," p. 56.
34. Quoted in Lynn Norment, "The Untold Story of How Tina and Mathew Knowles Created the Destiny's Child Gold Mine," *Ebony*, September 2001, p. 90.
35. Quoted in Norment, "The Untold Story of How Tina and Mathew Knowles Created the Destiny's Child Gold Mine," p. 90.
36. Quoted in Lorraine Ali, "A Date with Destiny," *Newsweek*, May 21, 2001, p. 54.
37. Knowles et al., *Soul Survivors*, p. 149.
38. Quoted in *Jet*, "Destiny's Child: Hot Young Divas Continue to Burn Up Music Charts," p. 58.
39. Knowles et al., *Soul Survivors*, p. 132.
40. Quoted in *Cosmopolitan*, "Beyoncé Knowles," p. 160.
41. Quoted in Samuels, "What Beyoncé Wants," p. 52.
42. David Browne, "Date with Destiny," *Entertainment Weekly*,

May 11, 2001, p. 77.

43. Farley, "Call of the Child," p. 128.

Chapter 4: Breaking into Acting

44. Quoted in Bracco, "Destiny's Child," p. 84.
45. Knowles et al., *Soul Survivors*, p. 216.
46. Knowles et al., *Soul Survivors*, p. 230.
47. Quoted in Samuels, "What Beyoncé Wants," p. 52.
48. Quoted in Paul Fischer, "Destiny's Child Superstar Heads to a Golden Big Screen Debut," *Film Monthly*. www.filmmonthly.com/Profiles/Articles/BeyoncéKnowles/BeyoncéKnowles.html.
49. Quoted in Samuels, "What Beyoncé Wants," p. 52.
50. Quoted in Lynn Norment, "Beyoncé Heats Up Hollywood!" *Ebony*, July 2002, p. 36.
51. Quoted in Samuels, "What Beyoncé Wants," p. 52.
52. Lisa Schwarzbaum, "Radical Cheek," *Entertainment Weekly*, August 2, 2002, p. 45.
53. Quoted in Samuels, "What Beyoncé Wants," p. 52.
54. Quoted in Fischer, "Destiny's Child Superstar Heads to a Golden Big Screen Debut."
55. Quoted in Carissa Rosenberg, "Above and Beyoncé," *CosmoGirl!* September 2002, p. 139.
56. Quoted in Rosenberg, "Above and Beyoncé," p. 139.
57. Quoted in Samuels, "What Beyoncé Wants," p. 52.

Chapter 5: Solo Sensation

58. Quoted in Karen Bliss, "Beyoncé Gets Dangerous," *Rolling Stone*, November 12, 2002. www.rollingstone.com/news/story/593655/beyonce_gets_dangerous.
59. Leah Rozen, "The Fighting Temptations," *People*, September 29, 2003, p. 33.
60. Quoted in Robinson, "Above and Beyoncé," p. 336.
61. Quoted in Robinson, "Above and Beyoncé," p. 336.
62. Neil Drumming, "Knowles No Bounds," *Entertainment Weekly*, June 27, 2003, p. 135.
63. Quoted in Robinson, "Above and Beyoncé," p. 336.

64. Quoted in Toure, "A Woman Possessed," *Rolling Stone*, March 4, 2004, p. 38.
65. Toure, "A Woman Possessed," p. 38.
66. Quoted in Robinson, "Above and Beyoncé," p. 336.
67. Quoted in *Jet*, "Destiny's Child: Reunites for New Album After Solo Successes," December 6, 2004, p. 60.
68. Chuck Arnold, "Destiny's Child: Destiny Fulfilled," *People*, November 22, 2004, p. 47.
69. Tom Sinclair, "A Dull Date with Destiny," *Entertainment Weekly*, November 26, 2004, p. 117.
70. Quoted in Toure, "A Woman Possessed," p. 38.

Chapter 6: Following Her Destiny

71. Leah Rozen and Nicholas White, "Movies," *People*, February 20, 2006, p. 33.
72. Jeannine Amber, "Beyoncé's Destiny," *Essence*, October 2005, p. 158.
73. Quoted in Amber, "Beyoncé's Destiny," p. 158.
74. Quoted in *Jet*, "Destiny's Child Announces Break Up," July 4, 2005, p. 36.
75. Quoted in *Jet*, "Destiny's Child Announces Break Up," p. 36.
76. Quoted in Robinson, "Above and Beyoncé," p. 336.
77. Quoted in Amber, "Beyoncé's Destiny," p. 158.
78. Quoted in Robinson, "Above and Beyoncé," p. 336.
79. Quoted in Amber, "Beyoncé's Destiny," p. 158.
80. Quoted in Karen S. Schneider and Jessica Herndon, "Take a Bow," *People*, September 26, 2005, p. 21.
81. Robinson, "Above and Beyoncé," p. 336.
82. Amber, "Beyoncé's Destiny," p. 158.
83. Quoted in Robinson, "Above and Beyoncé," p. 336.
84. Quoted in Amber, "Beyoncé's Destiny," p. 158.
85. Quoted in Brandee J. Tecson, "Beyoncé Slimming Down and 'Completely Becoming Deena,'" MTV Movies. www.mtv.com/movies/news/articles/1523138/02030226/story.jhtml.
86. Quoted in Tecson, "Beyoncé Slimming Down and 'Completely Becoming Deena.'"
87. Quoted in Robinson, "Above and Beyoncé," p. 336.

88. Quoted in Fametastic, "Beyoncé Knowles Loses 20 Pounds for Dreamgirls Role." http://fametastic.co.uk/archive/20060525/1329/beyonce-knowles-loses-20-pounds-for-dreamgirls-role.

89. Quoted in Foxnews.com, "Oscars 2007? 'Dreamgirls.'" www.foxnews.com/story/0,2933,196314,00.html.

90. Quoted in Amber, "Beyoncé's Destiny," p. 158.

1981

Beyoncé Knowles is born on September 4 in Houston, Texas.

1988

Beyoncé's parents enroll her in dance class. She enjoys performing so much that her parents begin entering her in talent competitions.

1990

Beyoncé becomes a member of the group Girl's Tyme.

1992

Girl's Tyme performs on the national television show *Star Search* but loses. Mathew Knowles becomes the manager of a new group featuring his daughter and several other girls.

1995

A recording contract is signed with Elektra Records, but the deal falls through soon after the girls begin recording their first album.

1996

Columbia Records signs the group to a contract, and they name themselves Destiny's Child.

1997

The single "No, No, No" is released and makes it to the top of *Billboard*'s R&B/Hip-Hop chart the next year.

1998

The group's first album, *Destiny's Child*, is released.

1999

Destiny's Child releases its second album, *The Writing's on the Wall*. It debuts at number six on the *Billboard* 200 album chart. In December, LaTavia Roberson and LaToya Luckett ask that Mathew Knowles no longer manage them.

2000

Destiny's Child replaces Luckett and Roberson with Michelle Williams and Farrah Franklin. Franklin leaves the group after a few months, and Destiny's Child regroups as a trio.

2001

The album *Survivor* is released by Destiny's Child. The group's members agree to take a break and try some solo projects. Beyoncé takes the lead in MTV's *Carmen: A Hip Hopera*.

2002

Beyoncé takes the role of Foxxy Cleopatra in *Austin Powers in Goldmember*, starring Mike Myers.

2003

The Fighting Temptations, with Cuba Gooding Jr., is Beyoncé's second big-screen effort. She releases her first solo album, *Dangerously in Love*.

2004

Beyoncé and the other members of Destiny's Child reunite to record *Destiny Fulfilled*.

2005

Destiny's Child releases its final album, goes on tour to promote it, and announces that the group is breaking up to allow its members to pursue individual projects. Beyoncé signs a licensing agreement for a fashion line. Beyoncé gets a lead role in *Dreamgirls*.

2006

Beyoncé continues to pursue an acting career. She releases her second solo album, *B-Day*.

For Further Reading

Books

Geoffrey Horn, *Beyoncé*. Milwaukee: G. Stevens, 2006. A brief account of Beyoncé's rise to stardom.

Beyoncé Knowles, Kelly Rowland, Michelle Williams, and James Patrick Herman, *Soul Survivors: The Official Autobiography of Destiny's Child*. New York: HarperCollins, 2002. A firsthand account from Beyoncé and the other members of Destiny's Child about the group's formation and personnel changes.

Kathleen Tracy, *Beyoncé*. Hockessin, DE: Mitchell Lane, 2005. This easy-to-read book emphasizes the struggles Beyoncé went through as she pursued her dream of becoming a performer.

Web Sites

Beyoncé Online (www.beyonceonline.com). The singer's official Web site offers news, music, and video clips relating to Beyoncé and opportunities to buy her DVDs and other products.

Internet Movie Database (www.imdb.com). Search for Beyoncé to find the actress's acting credits as well as a list of her songs used in films. The site also contains a biography and photo gallery.

People (www.people.com). A search for Beyoncé brings up news about the star.

Entertainment Weekly (www.ew.com). Features the latest news about Beyoncé and other celebrities.

Terri Dougherty is a newspaper reporter who loves writing biographies and other books for children. *Beyoncé* is her tenth People in the News biography. She and her husband, Denis, live in Appleton, Wisconsin, with their three children, Kyle, Rachel, and Emily.